FIRST BIOGRAPHIES

Abigail Adams

Cassie Mayer

Heinemann Library
Chicago, Illinois

© 2008 Heinemann Library
a division of Reed Elsevier Inc.
Chicago, Illinois

Customer Service **888-454-2279**

Visit our Web site at **www.heinemannlibrary.com**

Photo research by Tracy Cummins and Tracey Engel.
Designed by Kimberly R. Miracle
Printed and bound in China by South China Printing Company

10 09 08 07
10 9 8 7 6 5 4 3 2 1

10 Digit ISBN: 1-4034-9971-3 (hc)   1-4034-9980-2 (pb)

Library of Congress Cataloging-in-Publication Data
Mayer, Cassie.
 Abigail Adams / Cassie Mayer.
    p. cm. -- (First biographies)
 Includes bibliographical references and index.
 ISBN 978-1-4034-9971-4 (hc) -- ISBN 978-1-4034-9980-6 (pb)
 1. Adams, Abigail, 1744-1818--Juvenile literature. 2. Presidents' spouses--United States--Biography--Juvenile literature. I. Title.
 E322.1.A38M365 2007
 973.4'4092--dc22
 [B]
                           2007009983

Acknowledgements
The author and publisher are grateful to the following for permission to reproduce copyright material: ©Alamy **pp. 11** (Gabe Palmer), **12** (William Owens); ©Art Resource **pp. 10, 19, 23a**; ©The Bridgeman Art Library **p. 9** (National Gallery of Art, Washington, D.C., USA); ©Corbis **pp. 18** (Bettmann), **21**; ©Getty Images **pp. 8** (Stock Montage), **20** (Time Life Pictures), **22** (Win McNamee); ©The Granger Collection **pp. 4, 7**; ©Library of Congress Prints and Photographs Division **p. 5**; ©Massachusetts Historical Society **pp. 6, 13, 14, 16**; ©North Wind Picture Archives **pp. 17, 23b**; ©Shutterstock **p. 15** (Anyka).

Cover image reproduced with permission of ©The Granger Collection. Back cover image reproduced with permission of ©Shutterstock (Anyka).

Every effort has been made to contact copyright holders of any material reproduces in this book.
Any omissions will be rectified in subsequent printings if notice is given to the publisher.

Contents

Introduction

Abigail Adams was a leader.
A leader helps change things.

Abigail helped change how women live in our country.

Early Life

Abigail was born in 1744.
She lived in Massachusetts.

When Abigail was little, many girls did not go to school.

Abigail did not go to school.

But Abigail's father wanted her to read.

Abigail loved to read and write.

She read books from her father's library.

Marriage

Abigail and John's House

Abigail married John Adams in 1764.

John Adams worked for the government.
The government makes rules for people.

Abigail's Letters

My Dearest Friend   Bristol May 19   1800

                              we reached this place at half after five
we found the old inhabitants gone, the new inn keepers name
Tombes, the people civil and obligeing. every thing very neat
Jackson drove very well, Farmer and Favorite lazy Traveller &
ceasar brisk. I am fully of the mind that a middle size Horse
travels with more ease to himself, and pleasure to the driver,.
we shall get on slowly. I had rather have the Horses want driving
than be hurching and flouncing. I hope you will be very carefull on
your journey not to take cold. I must recommend the warm bath
to you once or twice before you sit out on your journey. not hot
that will drive the Blood to the Head; but it cleans the Skin &
renders the persperation free. I wish you a pleasant journey. and
a speedy return   to your A Adams

John Adams traveled a lot.
Abigail wrote letters to him.

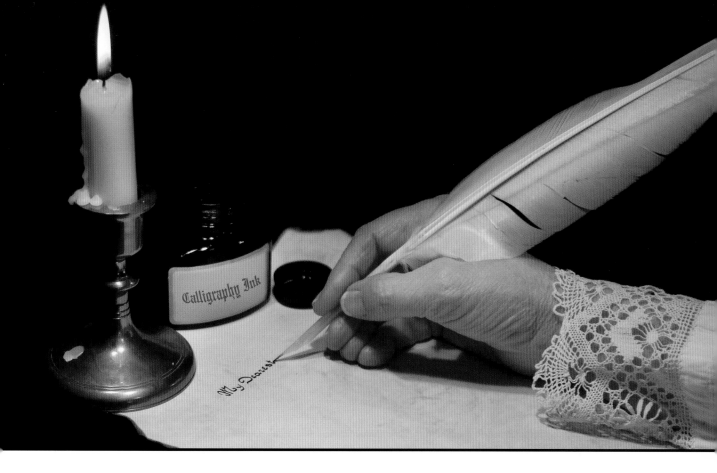

Abigail had many ideas about government. She wrote letters about these ideas.

Women's Right to Vote

[handwritten letter]

"remember the ladies"

Abigail wrote that women should have the right to vote.

The right to vote is one freedom that people have. To vote is to help decide who leads the government.

Women could not vote.

Women could not help decide who led the government.

John Adams became president of the United States in 1797.

Abigail became the First Lady of the
United States. A first lady is the wife of
the president.

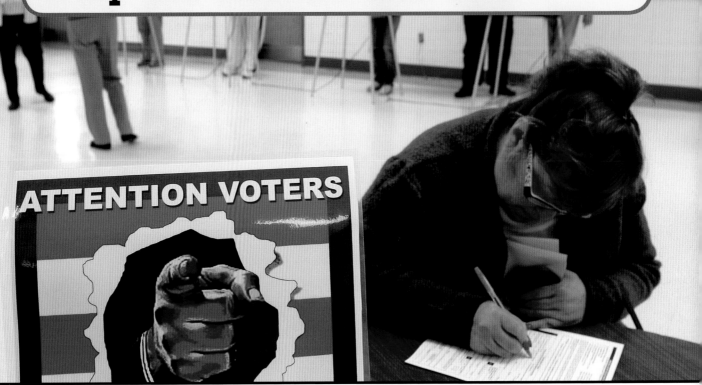

ATTENTION VOTERS

Abigail's ideas helped change the United States government. Women now have the same rights as men.

Picture Glossary

government a group of leaders who make rules for an area of land

vote tell who you would like to be leader. The person with the most votes becomes leader.

Timeline

1744 — born

1797 — becomes First Lady

1818 — dies

Index

Note to Parents and Teachers

This series introduces prominent historical figures, focusing on the significant events of each person's life and their impact on American society. Illustrations and primary sources are used to enhance students' understanding of the text.

The text has been carefully chosen with the advice of a literacy expert to enable beginning readers success while reading independently or with moderate support. An expert in the field of early childhood social studies curriculum was consulted to provide interesting and appropriate content.

You can support children's nonfiction literacy skills by helping students use the table of contents, headings, picture glossary, and index.